THE **NON-OBJECTIVE** WORLD

A NATIONAL TOURING EXHIBITION FROM
THE SOUTH BANK CENTRE 1992

LENDERS TO THE EXHIBITION

Cardiff, National Museum of Wales 46

Raymond Danowski 54

Edinburgh, Scottish National Gallery of Modern Art 62

Adrian Heath 28

Annely Juda Fine Art 4, 5, 7, 8, 20, 21, 22, 23, 24, 25, 26, 27, 33, 34, 36, 37, 48, 56, 59, 67, 68, 69, 70, 71, 72, 76

London, Trustees of the British Museum 1, 2, 18, 19, 30, 31, 32, 39, 40, 41, 42, 43, 44, 60, 61, 63

London, Government Art Collection 15

London, Tate Gallery 3

London, The Board of Trustees of the Victoria and Albert Museum 64

Manchester, Whitworth Art Gallery, University of Manchester 45

Henry Moore Foundation 49, 50

Norwich, University of East Anglia 6, 9, 13, 14, 17, 29, 38, 51, 65, 66, 73

Paule Vézelay's Family 74, 75

Wakefield Art Gallery 16

Nina Williams 10, 11, 12

Private Collections 35, 47, 52, 53, 55, 57, 58

Books are to be returned on or before
the last date below.

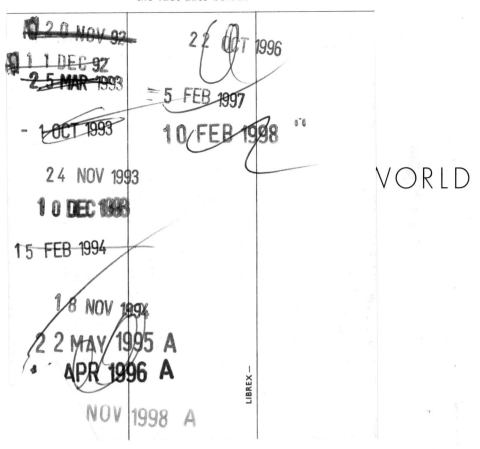
VORLD

EXHIBITION TOUR

Kettle's Yard, Cambridge, 6 June – 19 July 1992

Glynn Vivian Art Gallery, Swansea, 25 July – 6 September 1992

Walker Art Gallery, Liverpool, 18 September – 25 October 1992

Abbot Hall, Kendal, 31 October 1992 – 3 January 1993

A National Touring Exhibition from The South Bank Centre
Exhibition selected by Annely Juda
Exhibition organised by Ann Jones
Assisted by Leigh Markopoulos
Education Officer Helen Luckett
Catalogue designed by Crispin Rose-Innes Limited
Printed in England by Pale Green Press
Photographs by Michael Brandon-Jones, Geremy Butler, Sarah Quick
© The South Bank Centre 1992
ISBN 185332 085 4

A *full list of* Arts *Council and South Bank Centre publications may be obtained from:*
Art Publications, South Bank Centre, Royal Festival Hall, London SE1 8XX

Cover IVAN KLIUN **Untitled** 1922, Annely Juda Fine Art (cat. no. 21)

Inside front cover **Van Diemen Gallery**, Berlin 1922. Left to right: David Shterenberg (commissar of the exhibition), D. Maryanov (propaganda agent), Nathan Altman (artist), Naum Gabo

CONTENTS

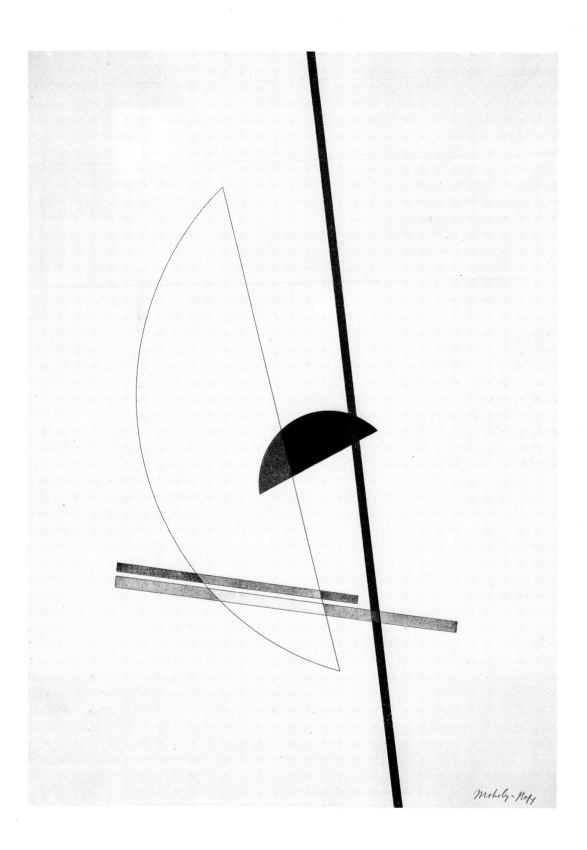

FOREWORD

The term 'non-objective' describes art which has no representational subject matter and is created from purely pictorial elements. The works in this exhibition provide insights into the exploration of the non-objective from its emergence in modern art around 1914 until the outbreak of the Second World War. As well as the work of Russian pioneers there are also paintings, sculptures, drawings and prints by their contemporaries and successors in western Europe.

The selection is drawn entirely from collections in Britain. There are very few important works by artists such as El Lissitzky, Malevich, Moholy-Nagy, Mondrian and Popova in British collections, and we are particularly grateful to the museums and private collectors who have agreed to lend.

Through the series of distinguished and well-researched exhibitions that she has held in her gallery over many years, Annely Juda has been responsible for introducing non-objective work to many people in this country. We are indebted to her for selecting the exhibition and for lending works from her collection.

The many strands in the emergence and development of geometrical abstract art are skilfully laid out in an essay by Martin Hammer of Edinburgh University and Christina Lodder of the University of St Andrews. We are also grateful for their help with other aspects of the exhibition.

We are delighted that the artists Adrian Heath and Richard Deacon have agreed to describe their personal responses to some of the works in the exhibition. David Fraser Jenkins, Adrian Glew, Anthony Griffiths, Jeremy Lewison, Margaret Pedley, Veronica Sekules and many others have contributed advice and assistance.

Joanna Drew
Director,
Hayward and Regional Exhibitions

Ann Jones
Exhibition Organiser

LÁSZLÓ MOHOLY-NAGY **Konstruktionen** 1923, Trustees of the British Museum (cat. no. 44)

THE **ABSTRACT** UTOPIA

THE INVENTION OF ABSTRACT ART

The type of art in this exhibition has been variously categorised as geometric abstraction, constructivism, or as non-objective or non-figurative art. Such terms are intended to distinguish the complete absence of representational subject-matter from the process of 'abstracting', or artistically transforming a still legible image. Yet 'abstract' remains the most common description of paintings and sculptures that emphatically resist our natural disposition to read works of art in terms of some specific imagery from our wider experience. This dual sense of abstract is confusing. But in actuality, critical labels are not very helpful when it comes to confronting particular works.

For a spectator unfamiliar with abstract art, the paintings and sculptures in this exhibition might well appear alarmingly simple, lacking in visual appeal, let alone meaning or outside reference. In these circumstances, grasping at conceptual handles is far less important than a simple willingness to look at the objects for a length of time, observing one's sensations and responses. One might then compare different works and artists, and hence the range of possibilities and variations available within such apparently restricted resources. For the works on show are built up, in the main, from lines and planes alone. The resulting compositions tend to be clear and precise in their overall structure, exploiting contrasts of colour, texture, shape and direction between these elementary components. The works may look highly impersonal and preconceived, the very opposite of the Wordsworthian idea of art as a spontaneous overflow of powerful feeling. If such art offends a Romantic sensibility, it might seem, on the other hand, to restate quintessentially 'classical' values: order, repose, simplicity and restraint, purity of form and harmony of proportion. A Mondrian, for instance, requires measured contemplation for its full subtleties to become apparent. Such formal appreciation requires no background knowledge and is appropriate to the highly aesthetic decisions about placement, strength of colour and so forth, that the making of the works certainly involved, notwithstanding their 'mathematical' look.

Ever since antiquity itself, such qualities as order and simplicity have commonly been invested with more metaphorical resonances[1]. Thus in the later eighteenth century, David's austere Neo-classicism embodied not only an aesthetic rejection of the over-elaborate Rococo style, but also a moral impulse to deflect art from frivolity and entertainment to a loftier didactic purpose, as in his stern assertion of the claims of civic duty over private feeling in the *Oath of the Horatii* 1784-5. A similar high-mindedness surfaced in early abstract art, in the analogous context of the political crisis and revolutionary aspirations of the 1910s. The pioneers of

ALEXANDER RODCHENKO **Untitled** 1919, Annely Juda Fine Art (cat. no. 59)

WASSILY KANDINSKY **Kleine Welten XI** 1922
Trustees of the British Museum (cat. no. 19)

abstract art were at pains to emphasise, in their extensive theoretical writings, that pure forms and colours constituted a more effective means than legible imagery to communicate ideas and emotions to the viewer. They saw an inextricable connection between abstract form and profundity or universality of meaning. The problem was how to create meaningful abstract images that avoided mere decorativeness, or 'the danger of ornament', in the words of Wassily Kandinsky, who is often seen as the earliest practitioner and theorist of abstraction.

Kandinsky's own solution, however, unlike those of most of his contemporaries, did not involve a process of stripping away, rather the pursuit of a rich pictorial drama. In his paintings from around 1910 to the outbreak of war in 1914, Kandinsky often worked with imagery of the Apocalypse, which he increasingly disguised or 'veiled' by generalising forms and accentuating marks, lines and patches of colour. The emotional charge of his original themes survives, however, in the visual dissonances and structural freedom of his compositions. Since the late nineteenth century, artists and critics had talked about art aspiring to the condition of music, with its autonomy of form and expressive directness. The qualities of Kandinsky's paintings recalled more specifically the 'atonal' musical innovations of his friend Schoenberg. In 1913 Kandinsky stated:

> Painting is like a thundering collision of different worlds that are destined in and through conflict to create that new world called the work. Technically, every work of art comes into being in the same way as the cosmos – by means of catastrophes, which ultimately create out of the cacophony of the various instruments that symphony we call the music of the spheres. The creation of the work of art is the creation of the world.[2]

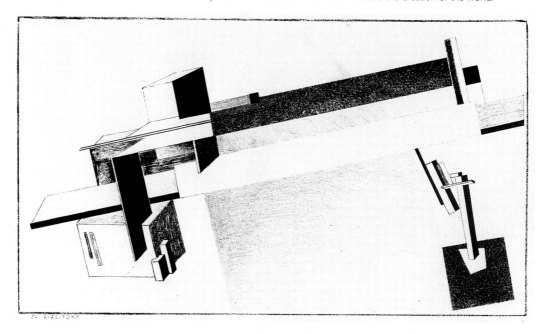

EL LISSITZKY **Proun 1A** 1919-21, Trustees of the British Museum (cat. no. 30)

In his treatise *On the Spiritual in Art*, published in 1912, Kandinsky argued that the artist should obey his intuition or 'inner necessity' in order to create works embodying spiritual values that would counteract the materialism of contemporary society[3]. He attempted to correlate different colours with particular psychological and emotional effects and also with specific forms and even musical sounds. Unusually, Kandinsky arrived at this vision of a completely abstract art without reference to Cubism. Kandinsky's later use of a more lucid geometry mainly reflected his response to the work of Kazimir Malevich, following Kandinsky's return to his native Russia after the outbreak of the First World War.

For other artists, the elimination of subject matter seemed the logical next step beyond pre-war Cubism and Futurism, which in turn had effected such a radical break from the Western naturalistic tradition. In Russia, for example, Malevich experimented for several years with the new ideas emanating from the West, such as geometric simplification of an image, the evocation of motion or the passage of time through multiplied contours, and an increasing emphasis on the autonomy of pictorial elements

Installation of the 0.10 exhibition St Petersburg 1915

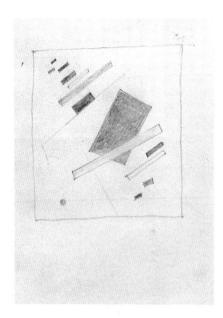

KAZIMIR MALEVICH **Suprematist Composition**
c.1916, Annely Juda Fine Art (cat. no. 33)

EL LISSITZKY **Proun, Unnumbered** 1919-21
Trustees of the British Museum (cat. no. 32)

and the identity of the painting as a flat surface rather than as a window onto a fictive world. In December 1915, at the Last Futurist Exhibition 0.10 (Zero-Ten), Malevich revealed a dramatic breakthrough, when he exhibited a roomful of totally abstract works comprising flatly painted planes of colour on white grounds. At one extreme, he placed a large black square in the centre of a square canvas, implying an artistic *tabula rasa*; at the other, he devised complex organisations from shapes varied in colour, scale and geometric regularity. The latter paintings in particular are richly suggestive of space and movement (eg. cat. no. 35). Malevich's style was widely emulated in Russia and acted as a catalyst for further innovation by such figures as Ivan Kliun, Alexander Rodchenko, Lyubov Popova, El Lissitzky and Nikolai Suetin.

At the same time as his exhibition, Malevich published a manifesto entitled 'From Cubism and Futurism to Suprematism'[4]. With a rhetoric to match Kandinsky's, he announced: 'I transformed myself in the zero of form and emerged from nothing to creation, that is to Suprematism, to the new realism in painting – to non-objective creation'. He characterised Suprematism as 'the pure art of painting', in which pictorial elements have their own reality, in contrast to the 'old realism' of imitation. Yet this did not mean that Malevich was only interested in formal effects for their own sake. He asserted, for example, that the new artistic language encapsulated the essential spirit of the contemporary world of speed and machinery. The Italian Futurists inspired his affirmation of the modern world, but he felt that, in practice, their art had been limited by its descriptive approach: '... in pursuing the form of aeroplanes or automobiles, we shall always be anticipating new cast-off forms of technical life ...'. For Malevich, it was necessary to create a more abstract equivalent:

> The artist can be a creator only when the forms in his pictures have nothing in common with nature. For art is the ability to construct, not on the interrelation of form and colour, and not on an aesthetic basis of beauty in composition, *but on the basis of weight, speed and the direction of movement.*

There are certain affinities between Suprematism and the definitive Neo-plasticism of Piet Mondrian. From around 1921 Mondrian employed only the elementary means of straight vertical and horizontal black lines, intersecting at right angles, enclosing flatly applied rectangles of white, occasionally grey, and the primary colours of red, yellow and blue. The clarity of design and self-effacing technique recall Malevich, but the dynamism and spatial openness of the Russian's paintings contrast markedly with the emphatic flatness and frontality of Mondrian's work, and his persistent avoidance of diagonal elements. Instead of an oscillating focus between the surface design and implied depth, Mondrian's paintings involve a different kind of interplay between relationships of shape and colour within the self-contained composition and more expansive suggestions of planes and lines continuing laterally beyond the physical edges.

IVAN KLIUN **Untitled** 1920, Annely Juda Fine Art (cat. no. 20)

LYUBOV POPOVA **Space-Force Construction** *c.*1920-1, Private Collection (cat. no. 57)

NIKOLAI SUETIN **Untitled** 1924-6, Annely Juda Fine Art (cat. no. 67)

Such visual distinctions correspond to the different meanings each wished his work to carry. Like Kandinsky, Mondrian was attracted to the esoteric mysticism of Theosophy and as early as 1909 he envisaged that art could 'provide a transition to the finer regions, which I call the spiritual realm'[5]. A lattice of horizontal and vertical accents already characterised the paintings Mondrian had made in Paris under the influence of the Cubists. Back in his native Holland during the war, this visual structure increasingly subsumed his depicted subject-matter, as in the Pier and Ocean series (eg. cat. no. 48). This direction was certainly reinforced by the experiments of Mondrian's artist friends with whom he formed the De Stijl group in 1917, including Theo van Doesburg and Bart van der Leck. In addition, Mondrian was reading Schoenmaekers, a Dutch philosopher, who argued in such books as *Principles of Plastic Mathematics* (1916) that the polarity of vertical and horizontal embodied the essential dualities at the heart of creation: the individual and the universal, mind and matter, male and female and so on. Such thinking gave Mondrian confidence in the symbolic resonance of pure pictorial contrasts and he asserted in 1917 that 'Art — although an end in itself like religion — is the means through which we can know the universal and contemplate it in plastic form'[6]. The quality he most insistently claimed for his abstract paintings was 'dynamic equilibrium'. In its pursuit, the possibilities for generating taut asymmetrical arrangements of colour and line proved considerable, and Mondrian produced an extraordinarily rich body of work within the 'limitations' of a pictorial language whose very structure was, for the artist, suffused with 'universal' meanings. As in the case of Malevich, Mondrian's paintings stand out from those of his many followers by virtue not only of their compositional inventiveness and strength but also of the surprising beauty of their surfaces, as in the layered build-up of the white areas to prevent them seeming to recede behind the black grid. Both painters lose much in reproduction.

BART VAN DER LECK
Watercolour no. 390 1916-32
University of East Anglia (cat. no. 29)

ART INTO LIFE

The artists, architects and designers of the De Stijl group aspired to extend its elementary organisational principles into the wider visual environment. As van Doesburg stated, 'the consciousness of the new plasticism implies co-operation of all the plastic arts in order to attain a pure monumental style on the basis of balanced relationships'[7]. The very name they chose denoted that they had arrived at *the* style for their age, the inevitable artistic correlative to progress in science, technology and society at large.

For such idealistic artists and intellectuals throughout Europe, the Russian Revolution of 1917 seemed to promise the arrival of Utopia. The overthrow of the Tsarist autocracy and the establishment of a communist state had a particular impact on Russian artists. During the ensuing three years, while the Civil War was being fought, the avant-garde ran artistic

PIET MONDRIAN **Composition with Red, Yellow and Blue** 1927, Private Collection (cat. no. 47)

affairs and were involved in agitational and propaganda projects such as decorating the cities for the revolutionary festivals and designing posters. Often the formal language of Suprematism was applied to these new tasks, identifying artistic radicalism with the wider political and social revolution. Likewise, Vladimir Tatlin declared that 'what happened from the social aspect in 1917 was realised in our work as pictorial artists in 1914 when "materials, volume and construction" were accepted as our foundation'[8]. In May 1914 Tatlin had exhibited his first three-dimensional reliefs, inspired by the Cubist collages and constructions that he had seen in Paris that Spring. Soon, however, Tatlin's creations were totally abstract, exploring contrasts of materials and textures and more active relationships between the relief and its spatial environment. Thus *Corner Counter-Relief* of 1915 (shown here in Martyn Chalk's reconstruction, cat. no. 71) is built up around two intersecting metal planes suspended across the corners of a room.

Tatlin was an enthusiastic convert to the Bolshevik cause, as was manifest in his extraordinary *Model for a Monument to the Third International*, first exhibited in late 1920 (see p. 38). He intended the final structure to be a third as high again as the Eiffel Tower and to straddle the River Neva in St Petersburg. The external iron framework, spiralling upwards on a diagonal axis, created a powerful image of dynamism and progress. Within it were to be suspended three enormous glazed volumes (rotating at various speeds) that were to house the different bodies of the Third International, an organisation devoted to promoting world revolution. The Tower was to combine the geometric clarity of the new abstract art with industrial materials and technology, synthesising 'the principles of architecture, sculpture and painting' and 'uniting purely artistic forms with utilitarian intentions'[9]. The emphasis on practical application, and on a 'machine-age' aesthetic appropriate to a workers' state, made the Tower a paradigm of new possibilities for the Russian avant-garde.

Inspired by Tatlin's call for artists to 'take control over the forms encountered in everyday life'[10]. Alexei Gan, Alexander Rodchenko, Varvara Stepanova and others began in March 1921 to describe themselves as Constructivists, the first appearance of a term widely used thereafter. The group, which pledged its allegiance to 'marxist materialism', rejected art as a bourgeois commodity, replacing it with 'intellectual production', which would harness artistic skills to designing everyday items for industrial manufacture and so help in the creation of the new socialist environment[11]. In practice, because no advanced industrial base existed in Russia, the group went on to design furniture, theatre sets and exhibitions and to exploit photomontage and bold layouts in their advertising and propaganda work. By 1922 other artists like Popova and Gustav Klucis had come to share the Constructivists' objectives. Popova and Stepanova, convinced that 'a cotton print is as much a product of artistic culture as a painting'[12] worked at the First Textile Print Factory in Moscow, applying

Reconstruction by Martyn Chalk 1987 of Tatlin's **Counter-Relief** c.1917, Annely Juda Fine Art (cat. no. 72)

Reconstruction by Martyn Chalk 1982 of Tatlin's **Corner Counter-Relief** 1915
Annely Juda Fine Art (cat. no. 71)

their abstract pictorial language to devising textile designs for mass production. In accordance with the Constructivists' industrial imperative, traditional floral patterns were discarded in favour of the 'geometricisation of form'[13]. The designs were based on economical combinations of one or more colours and simple geometric forms. In a typical example (cat. no. 58) Popova interlaced yellow and pink circles with vertical black lines of varying thickness, reinforcing the sense of spatial dynamism through the introduction of a diagonal break in the pattern.

INTERNATIONAL CONSTRUCTIVE ART

The Russian Constructivists' renunciation of art for practical design was a specifically Russian development, conditioned by the actual political circumstances in which the artists found themselves. At the same time, in the West, geometric abstract art began to crystallise as an international tendency and aesthetic. To an extent, the principal styles had already been formed, and the period from 1922 to the Second World War is characterised more by consolidation, cross-fertilisation and diffusion than by any startling innovations.

For the first decade, the principal focus of activity was Germany. Knowledge of both De Stijl and recent Russian developments proved a key catalyst. Such work provided a more positive 'constructive' alternative to the nihilistic mentality of the Dada movement, which had emerged in response to the horrors of the war and the cynical materialism of the societies involved. The first Russian Art Exhibition, which opened at the van Diemen Gallery in Berlin in October 1922, included Suprematist

LYUBOV POPOVA **Textile Design** 1924
Private Collection (cat. no. 58)

OBMOKhU **exhibition**, Moscow, May 1921, including work by Rodchenko and other members of the First Working Group of Constructivists

KURT SCHWITTERS **Collage** 1930, Trustees of the British Museum (cat. no. 63)

Probedruck   Moholy-Nagy

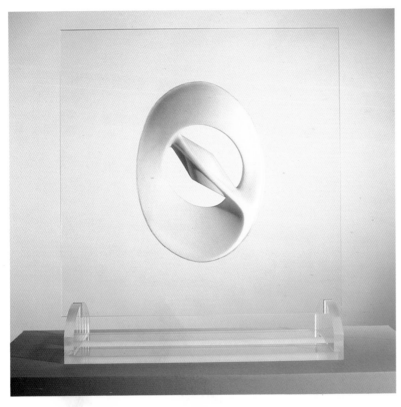

NAUM GABO **Construction in Space with Rose Marble Carving** 1966, Nina Williams (cat. no. 12)

works and constructions by Tatlin, Rodchenko and Gabo. Such artistic innovations were identified with the progressive ideology of post-revolutionary Russia and with 'the art of the material culture of the technical age'[14]. Moreover, El Lissitzky and Gabo had come to Berlin themselves in 1921 and 1922 respectively. The former was a tireless promoter and organiser, forging links with the De Stijl artists and with avant-garde groups in Germany, including Dadaists such as Hans Richter and Kurt Schwitters, who subsequently converted, so to speak, to International Constructivism. In the editorial of a new magazine *Veshch* (*Object*), which 'stands for a new way of thinking and unites the leaders of the new art in nearly all countries', Lissitzky succinctly defined the emerging aesthetic:

> The new art is founded not on a subjective, but on an objective basis. This, like science, can be described with precision and is by nature constructive. It unites not only pure art, but all those who stand at the frontier of the new culture. The artist is companion to the scholar, the engineer and the worker[15].

NAUM GABO **Construction in Space with Balance on Two Points** 1925, Yale University Art Gallery, New Haven, gift of H Wade White 1933 in memory of Joseph M Hirschman

By the mid 1920s, such views had become the common currency of groups in Holland, Germany, Czechoslovakia, Poland and the important set of artists who had left Hungary following the abortive revolution of 1919. It was László Moholy-Nagy who most vividly demonstrated the repudiation of subjectivity and personal touch. In 1922 he dictated over the telephone to an enamel factory the colours and composition of three

LÁSZLÓ MOHOLY-NAGY **Konstruktionen** 1923, Trustees of the British Museum (cat. no. 39)

paintings, using a colour chart and squared paper. A preoccupation with effects of transparency underlay the paintings of El Lissitzky, Moholy-Nagy and their many followers as well as Gabo's remarkable spatial constructions in glass and plastic. Over and above their formal elegance, such works make clear allusions to the materials and structural economy of engineering, to the conceptual precision of mathematical thinking (a model of rational analysis for artist and social planner alike), and also perhaps to the supplanting in current scientific theory of received notions of solid matter surrounded by empty space, in favour of new concepts of atomic structure and the physicists' 'fields' of force and energy. Gabo would later invoke:

> ... a world which is pictured to us as a conglomeration of oscillating electrons, protons, neutrons, particles which behave like waves, which in turn behave like particles. If the scientist is permitted to picture to us an image of an electron which under certain conditions has less than zero energy ... – why, may I ask, is not the contemporary artist to be permitted to search for and bring forward an image of the world more in accordance with the achievements of our developed mind ...[16]

The proselytising of van Doesburg in Weimar, and the appointment of Moholy-Nagy to run the Bauhaus Foundation Course, signalled a decisive aesthetic shift at the famous art school. Expressionism was abandoned in favour of a more affirmative attitude towards the machine and industry, epitomised by Gropius' slogan of 1923 – 'Art and Technology – a New Unity'. The practical results were such classics of modern design as Marcel Breuer's tubular steel furniture and Kurt Wagenfeld's lamps. Clearly the full realisation of 'Constructivist' principles of design depended not merely on idealism, but also on the entrepreneurial ethos and availability of materials and technology under German capitalism. In the school's painting studios, meanwhile, such figures as Kandinsky, Paul Klee and Josef Albers expounded the practical and theoretical possibilities of abstraction in art, which in turn fuelled the inventions of designers. The series of Bauhaus books, produced under the editorship of Moholy-Nagy, gave wide circulation to the ideas of Malevich, Mondrian, Kandinsky, Moholy-Nagy himself and others.

Publications and exhibitions led to an increased awareness of abstract art. In the 1930s, the most inspirational figure was undoubtedly Mondrian, who had been working in Paris since 1919. During the first half of the decade, indeed, Paris became the dominant centre of activity for abstract painters and sculptors. New organisations were formed there such as Cercle et Carré (Circle and Square) in 1930 and the more significant Abstraction-Création – Art Non-Figuratif, a notably international and comprehensive grouping that lasted from 1931 to 1936 and included figures such as Sonia Delaunay-Terk, César Domela, Naum Gabo, Barbara Hepworth, Auguste Herbin, František Kupka, Piet Mondrian, Ben Nicholson, Sophie Täuber-Arp and Friedrich Vordemberge-Gildewart. At

CHARLES BIEDERMAN **Untitled 3** 1936
University of East Anglia (cat. no. 6)

FLORENCE HENRI **Composition** 1927, University of East Anglia (cat. no. 14)

1927   F. Henri.

FRIEDRICH VORDEMBERGE-GILDEWART **Composition No. 60** 1931, Annely Juda Fine Art (cat. no. 76)

this stage, younger artists began to build upon the achievements of the 'pioneers', often progressing from reductive purity to more complex types of organisation and a more 'organic' vocabulary of biomorphic forms. Artists such as Jean Hélion and Paule Vézelay now looked to the example of the more abstract Surrealists such as Jean Arp (eg. cat. no. 3) and Miró. Indeed, Arp also became a member of Abstraction-Création. Both the composition and the title of his relief, *Constellation According to the Laws of Chance* c.1930, typify a concern to infuse abstraction with more poetic and improvisational qualities.

The background to this westward geographical shift was political. Abstract artists now found themselves less the force for social and intellectual progress to which they aspired, and more the victims of an aggressive anti-modernism on the part of totalitarian governments of both left and right. In the Soviet Union, the avant-garde was increasingly marginalised, even before the Party's imposition of Socialist Realism as the state's official artistic ideology after 1932. Against this backdrop, the later careers of many of the Suprematist and Constructivist artists offer a tragic spectacle. Likewise, the Nazis' advent to power in 1933 led to the closure of the Bauhaus and to the mass exodus of experimental artists such as Gabo, Domela and Kandinsky, who all gravitated to Paris. Yet despite the worsening political prospects, defenders of abstraction retained a resolutely idealistic tone, as in this 1935 evocation of 'the art of the new classless society':

SONIA DELAUNAY-TERK **Projet de Tissu** 1925
Annely Juda Fine Art (cat. no. 7)

PAULE VÉZELAY **Worlds in Space** 1935
The artist's family (cat. no. 75)

27

WINIFRED NICHOLSON **Untitled** 1935-6
Raymond Danowski (cat. no. 54)

JOHN CECIL STEPHENSON **Untitled** 1937
University of East Anglia (cat. no. 65)

... you cannot build a new society without artists. The artists are waiting for their opportunity: abstract artists who are, in this time of transition, perfecting their formal sensibility, who will be ready, when the time comes, to apply their talents to the great work of reconstruction. That is not a work for romanticists ... Communism is realist, scientific, essentially classical.[17]

Surprisingly enough, this was written by an Englishman, the critic Herbert Read. For three or four years before hostilities erupted, London became the final European refuge of the abstract avant-garde. Native artists such as Barbara Hepworth, Ben Nicholson, Winifred Nicholson, Henry Moore and John Cecil Stephenson now responded enthusiastically to current developments in Paris. In 1935, under the aegis of the Seven and Five society, they were able to mount the first entirely abstract exhibition in England since the Vorticist group shows twenty years previously. Ben Nicholson's white reliefs were perhaps the most distinctive contribution by an English artist, combining purity of shape and colour with the more ephemeral and ambiguous play of light and shadow on carved planes (eg. cat. no. 52). The highly simplified carvings of Barbara Hepworth (eg. cat. no. 15) had close affinities with Nicholson's reliefs.

Henry Moore, on the other hand, united stringing adapted from mathematical models with forms that evoke imagery of the human body and that frequently derive from his study of bones, shells and pebbles. In the year that he began his string sculpture (eg. cat. no. 49), he wrote:

BARBARA HEPWORTH **Conoid, Sphere and Hollow II** 1937
Government Art Collection (cat. no. 15)

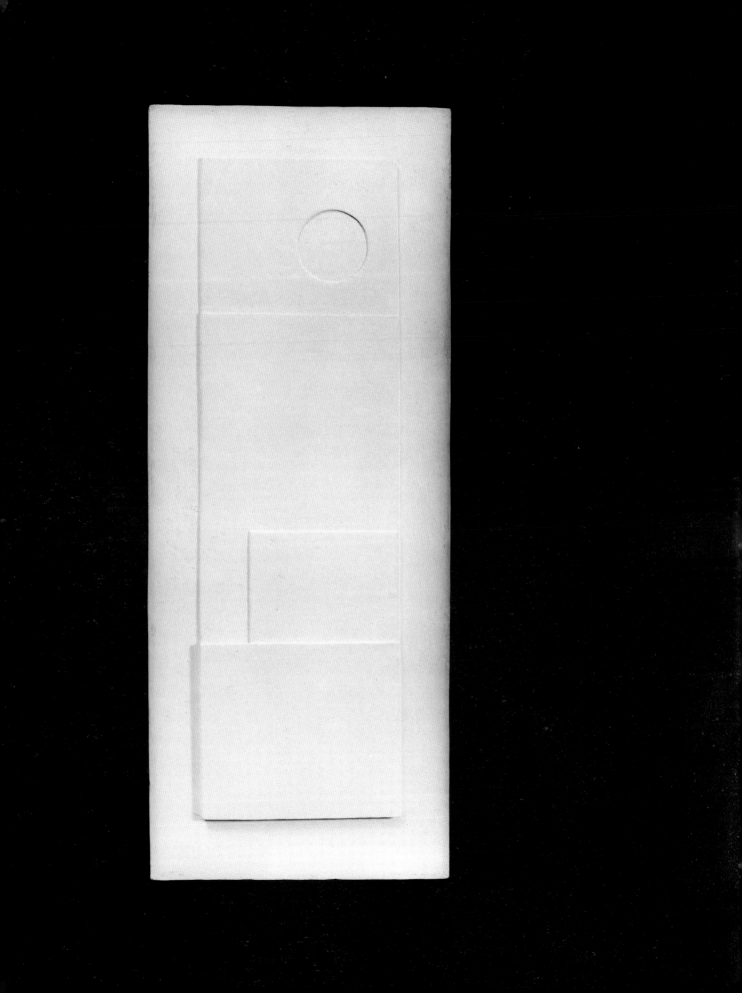

HENRY MOORE **Stringed Relief** 1937
Henry Moore Foundation (cat. no. 49)

The violent quarrel between the abstractionists and the surrealists seems to me quite unnecessary. All good art has contained both abstract and surrealist elements, just as it has contained both classical and romantic elements – order and surprise, intellect and imagination, conscious and unconscious. Both sides of the artist's personality must play their part.[18]

Alastair Morton's 'Constructivist Fabrics' project of 1937 represented a British continuation of the ideal of applying the new artistic language to everyday design. These endeavours were strongly reinforced by the arrival of European émigrés such as Gropius, Breuer and Moholy-Nagy, leading figures from the Bauhaus, followed by Gabo in 1936 and Mondrian in 1938. All would eventually move on to America, but for a time 'England seemed alive and rich – the centre of an international movement in architecture and art. We all seemed carried on the crest of this robust and inspiring wave of imaginative and creative energy' (Hepworth)[19].

Aside from the actual works, the most lasting monument to what is sometimes termed 'English Constructivism' was the volume *Circle*, a book-length 'International Survey of Constructive Art' produced in 1937 under the editorship of Gabo, Ben Nicholson and the architect Leslie Martin. The book contained work and writings by virtually all the leading architects and artists of the international 'constructive trend'. For all its optimism, *Circle* was, in a sense, the swansong of the artistic direction encapsulated in this exhibition. Individual artists carried on, of course, in the same vein, and, as a 'style', geometric abstraction has remained one significant option amongst many on the post-war scene. The extreme and uncompromising character of the work of the pioneering generations remains a compelling inspiration. Yet in terms of their own motivations, their art cannot be understood in isolation from utopian ideals which have come to seem increasingly remote, especially now, in the era of the final demise of Communism. Ultimately, looking at this type of art also entails an imaginative leap into the historical moment of its creation.

HENRY MOORE **Head** 1937
Henry Moore Foundation (cat. no. 50)

Martin Hammer and Christina Lodder

BEN NICHOLSON **1935 (white relief)**, Private Collection (cat. no. 52)

NOTES

1. Ernst H. Gombrich, 'Visual Metaphors of Value in Art' in **Meditations on a Hobby Horse**, Oxford, Phaidon 1971, pp. 12-29.

2. Wassily Kandinsky, 'Reminiscences' (1913) in Kenneth Lindsay and Peter Vergo (eds.), **Kandinsky. Complete Writings on Art**, London, Faber and Faber 1982, Vol.1, p. 373.

3. Wassily Kandinsky, 'On the Spiritual in Art' (1912) in **Kandinsky: Complete Writings on Art**, Vol.1, pp. 114-219.

4. Kazimir Malevich, 'From Cubism to Suprematism. The New Realism in Painting', in Kazimir Malevich, **Essays on Art 1915-1933**, London, Rapp and Whiting 1971, Vol.1, pp. 19-41. All the quotations in this paragraph are taken from this text.

5. Piet Mondrian, letter to the critic Israel Quierdo (1909) in Robert Welsh and J.M. Joosten (eds.), **Two Mondrian Sketchbooks 1912-1914**, Amsterdam, Meulenhoff International 1969, p. 10.

6. Piet Mondrian, 'The New Plastic in Painting' (1917) in Harry Holtzman and Martin S. James (eds.) **The New Art – The New Life: The Collected Writings of Piet Mondrian**, Boston, G.K. Hall & Co 1986, p. 42.

7. Theo van Doesburg, 'Notes on Monumental Art with reference to two fragments of a building (hall in holiday centre at Noordwijkerhout'), **De Stijl**, Vol.II, No.1, 1918, pp. 10-2 in Hans L.C. Jaffé, **De Stijl**, London, Thames and Hudson 1970, p. 99.

8. Vladimir Tatlin, T. Shapiro, I. Meerzon and P. Vinogradov, 'The Work Ahead of Us', **Eighth Congress of the Soviets: Daily Bulletin of the Congress VTsIK**, No. 13, 1 January 1921, in Stephen Bann (ed), **The Tradition of Constructivism**, London, Thames and Hudson 1974, pp. 12-4.

9. See Nikolai Punin, **Monument to the Third International**, Petrograd, IZO Narkompros, 1920 and Tatlin's declaration 'The Work Ahead of Us'.

10. Tatlin, 'The Work Ahead of Us'.

11. See 'Programme of the Working Group of Constructivists' in S.O. Khan-Magomedov, **Rodchenko: The Complete Work**, London, Thames and Hudson 1986, pp. 289-90.

12. Osip Brik, 'From Pictures to Textile Prints', **LEF**, No. 2, 1924, authors' translation. The text is given in full in John E. Bowlt (ed.), **Russian Art of the Avant-garde: Theory and Criticism 1902-1934**, London, Thames and Hudson 1988, pp. 244-9.

13. Varvara Stepanova, 'Concerning the position and tasks of the artist-constructor in the textile printing industry, in connection with work at a textile printing factory', cited by Christina Lodder, **Russian Constructivism**, London and Newhaven, Yale University Press 1983, p. 151.

14. Alfred Kemeny, 'Die abstrakte Gestaltung vom Suprematismus bis heute', **Das Kunstblatt**, No. 8, 1924, p. 248.

15. 'Statement by the Editors of Veshch/Gegenstand/Objet' in Bann, **The Tradition of Constructivism**, p. 63.

16. **Gabo: Constructions, Sculpture, Paintings, Drawings, Engravings**, London, Lund Humphries 1957, p. 176.

17. Herbert Read, 'What is Revolutionary Art?' in B. Rea (ed.), **Five on Revolutionary Art**, London 1935, pp. 21-2.

18. Henry Moore, 'Notes on Sculpture', reprinted in **Henry Moore, Sculpture and Drawing**, London, Lund Humphries 1944, p. xLii.

19. Barbara Hepworth, **A Pictorial Autobiography**, Tate Gallery, London 1978, p. 37.

JOHN CECIL STEPHENSON **Untitled**, c.1936/7
The Board of Trustees of the Victoria and Albert Museum (cat. no. 64)

34

A PAINTER'S VIEW

ADRIAN HEATH

My interest in Malevich and Rodchenko dates from 1949 when I came across reproductions of their work in Alfred Barr's *Cubism and Abstract Art*. My curiosity was aroused but not satisfied by those small black and white reproductions and Barr's summary text. I longed to see some original work, but I had to wait ten years until Bryan Robertson brought a retrospective of Malevich to the Whitechapel in 1959. Today the situation is very different; no young painter need feel himself deprived of knowledge about any artist of distinction. Large monographs with coloured reproductions abound, and the museums of the world put on travelling exhibitions accompanied by scholarly catalogues that cover their 'subject' from every angle. *The Non-Objective World* may not include more than a sampling of major works, but the drawings, studies and prints are as revealing of an artist's intention as the letters and journals of a writer.

In the past, certainly since the Renaissance, the prime object of drawing for the artist was to forge a link between himself and nature. The information that was gathered in this way went straight or indirectly into his painting. That this approach no longer applies to *The Non-Objective World*, the title of the exhibition makes clear.

To me, the drawings made by Mondrian between 1912 and 1918, of trees, the facades of buildings and the sea, are among the most rewarding of the twentieth century. We can watch him selecting and reducing from appearance until he arrives at the elements he needs to build these images of isolation and tranquillity. The number of drawings that Mondrian made after 1920 diminished dramatically; this is not surprising as he now started each canvas by drawing a grid of charcoal lines, a flexible structure that was constantly altered till finally he took up his paintbrush. Drawing played its part in the early development of every work, and his unfinished pictures reveal themselves as drawing in its purest form.

Malevich, during his Suprematist phase, chose to start working from the most basic conceptual elements: the square, the circle, the triangle and the quadrilateral. With such a battery of Euclidian form one might expect a geometric solution, but this was not his way. As with Mondrian and Nicholson, it was always Malevich's eye, or rather the spirit behind the eye that dictated the development of his work. His early pencil drawing of 1916, *Suprematist Composition*, is evidence of his new approach to this art of pure form. It seems to me to be an act of visualisation, tentative rather than casual. Having learned to respect the flatness of the pictorial surface (possibly from Cubist *papiers collés*) the paper in his drawings of this period is never covered with a gradated wash of colour to create atmosphere and spatial effect, and yet, paradoxically the simple pencil

KAZIMIR MALEVICH **Suprematist Composition** c.1920-2, Private Collection (cat. no. 35)

marks do generate a feeling of space and of the movement of forms in space. I see these drawings as a prelude to something else and their fulfilment is in the paintings. There is a dense finality about these canvases that only their physical presence can convey.

Speaking as a painter, I have always been fascinated by Mondrian's working methods, empirical procedures and execution. The craquelure that is evident in many of his canvasses is an indication of his repeated adjustments to attain the exact shade of white, and his use of 'scotch tape', a temporary expedient in thickening a black line so that his eye could make judgement, reveals an approach that owes nothing to calculation or pre-planning. It could even be said that Mondrian was an action painter working in slow motion. It is certain that he belonged to the category of artist who derives stimulus from contact with the medium, and to whom the execution of a work is a pleasure as well as a necessity. Nicholson was the same, he enjoyed carving down into his reliefs and he was stimulated by the risk of going too deep and the endless carving that would ensue to compensate for such a mistake.

I have still not seen Rodchenko's *Black on Black* that excited my curiosity so long ago, but I have seen other works by him from the same period. Their daring and their impatience has mellowed, defiantly rather than gracefully, into a timeless statement of intent. They are no longer outrageous but have become beautiful. As with Malevich, Rodchenko's paintings of these early years far outstrip the drawings of the same period. Perhaps the reverse could be said of El Lissitzky. His work on paper is far from tentative; clarity and subtlety in the distribution of tonal gradations are the hallmark of his drawings, and the precision is that of an engineering draughtsman. He is skilful at disguise and what at first glance may appear to be a two-dimensional design, will on inspection reveal enough information to make a three-dimensional construction. His work has always impressed me by its intelligence and sensitivity, but it totally lacks that mysterious authority inherent in a composition by Malevich or Mondrian. This essence must surely be generated by some artistic belief, some form of faith difficult to define.

Of course, the younger generation of Russian artists, equipped with ruler and compass, denied its existence. Indeed, by 1922 the ideals of Suprematism had been transformed into a basic design course with typography and photography to follow in order to clarify the message. It is not surprising that Gabo and Kandinsky baulked at this development and returned to Germany.

Adrian Heath – *British artist, born 1920*

Adrian Heath has been making abstract works of a painterly nature since the late 1940s. He played a leading role in British Constructivism in the 1950s and in 1953 he wrote *Abstract Art, its Origin and Meaning,* one of the first essays about abstraction to be published in Britain.

ADRIAN HEATH **Curved Forms: Yellow and Black** c.1954, The Artist

A SCULPTOR'S VIEW

LIVING IN A MATERIAL WORLD

RICHARD DEACON

It has sometimes been said that when Tatlin completed his *Model for a Monument to the Third International* it was carried through the streets by ox cart. The vaunting ambition of the proposal, the future it espoused and the belief in the transforming power of the social situation which caused it are poignantly contrasted with the lumbering transport of pre-Revolutionary Russia. The collapse of the Communist enterprise there and elsewhere, not before too long one might say, has seemed to be the final curtain call of that future, although Tatlin's star had long since fallen, hope abandoned. There is another story that concerns Tatlin. Some few years before, in 1914, the ex-sailor made his way to Paris and, hanging about in Picasso's studio, saw the reliefs he was then making. These odd bits of wood, paper, cloth, metal, material and paint formed the seed which, carried back to Russia, grew first into the counter-reliefs and finally into The *Model for a Monument to the Third International*. It's slightly para-doxical – though that is the way of these things – that the 'non-objective world' should have grown, in part, from Picasso's bits of tat. At the time the appearance of the reliefs must have been profoundly shocking, satu-rated as they are with their mundanity. It's a long step from those accu-mulations to Nicholson's *1935 (white relief)* which is almost, but not quite, immaterial, as if cut from some ethereal space.

Tatlin returned to Russia, assembling his first counter-reliefs in some-what the same fashion as Picasso, yet the difference is profound. Crudely, where one might say Picasso played with the space of representation, delighting in tripping between object and image, Tatlin began to see space itself as a material. The first counter-reliefs seem to splay an object out. Shape, shine, transparency, volume, texture and colour gather across their surfaces like a great question. Then in the corner-reliefs, awkwardly strung across or pushing out from the physical place in a room where planes meet, a balance is struck. Space and material substance are covalent (not equivalent since neither replaces the other). Rodin's great insight about sculpture being the art of the 'bump and the hollow' is given a surprising twist.

If 'not quite' immaterial is the way to describe Nicholson's relief, it's that 'not quite' which makes the link with Tatlin. The sense of the cut, smoothed and sanded hardboard lurks within our perception and is never displaced by the precise, deceptively gentle but insistent modulations for-ward and backwards over the surface.

'We deny volume as an expression of space' Gabo and Pevsner had written in their Realistic Manifesto of 1920, in part a blast against Tatlin

VLADIMIR TATLIN **Model for a Monument to the Third International** 1920

and Malevich. One imagines the Hampstead scene slightly later, with serious and modern-minded men and women trying to visualise a world of planes in the absence of volume, of space that was defined yet uncontained. The paradigm for this is Gabo's vibrating rod in the Tate Gallery, as radical as a corner-relief. The later Gabos, such as the one in this exhibition, seem to step back a little, to relax a bit. Seeing the *Construction in Space with Rose Marble Carving* the eye seems to swim, rolling gently dolphinlike around and in and out of the pierced stone, the body stilled, feeling a soft wash of spatial drifting.

Whilst Gabo's work has a certain magisterial authority, Barbara Hepworth's work of the 1930s reaches similar places, but more simply. There is an earlier work than those shown here which always catches me by surprise. Really it's just four marble pebbles on a plate. 'Look' one can almost hear it saying and it's impossible to know whether you look at the pebbles or between them. Of course a certain amount of this is a trick of the light, of the way marble responds to light. Not entirely, by a long way. *Conoid, Sphere and Hollow II* is a small work, a foot in each dimension. The three parts are all of the same white marble and all seem to be more or less equal. The named third part 'Hollow' is a negative though, and it is this negative part which supports, shelters and sustains the two positive volumes, in and out, like breathing.

Arp's slithery shapes have always been a bit oddball. Yet in a random universe you'd probably end up with something more like Arp and less like Gabo. We are supposed to believe that; were it truly random then neither is more likely. The 1920s and 1930s saw much playing around with chance and randomness; irrupting Dada evenings, Duchamp's standard stoppages etc. are all 'Spaniards in the works' of rationality. There is a certain irony in the title of Jean Arp's work in this exhibition, *Constellation According to the Laws of Chance*, chance and law seeming to sit on opposite fences and the laws of chance being the fool's gold of most gambling systems. Like Arp's 1931 *One Large Two Small*, absence of reason is taken as reason and we are distracted in our search for order. Or at least brought back to the slithery shapes in front of us.

I can imagine Henry Moore talking to Jean Arp, but I can't imagine him in that Hampstead room, visualising. I know no work by Henry Moore that does not come from a direct experience of a body, particularly throughout the 20s and 30s. If one were ever to describe a sculpture by Henry Moore with the words 'like breathing' one would mean 'like feeling one's chest rise and fall'. The string in his *Stringed Relief* does not so much describe a curved plane as draw parts together like sinew. However the absence of anatomy remains quite astonishing in the works which Henry Moore, in Unit One, made when he was closest to the Constructivist dialogue – the *Reclining Figure* like a set of bathroom scales from 1936 for example or the *Head* in green serpentine shown here.

RICHARD DEACON **Lock** 1990, The Artist

There is an astounding degree of objectification of the body in these works, an absence of interior. Any holes in the head are for looking, eating, hearing, smelling. There is no psychology. Although based on a body, the materiality of this view is not so far from Tatlin.

Richard Deacon – *British sculptor, born 1949*

Richard Deacon's sculptures are constructed or 'fabricated' rather than modelled or carved and in this sense they follow on in the tradition of Vladimir Tatlin. They do not represent objects from the natural world and are made from a variety of materials including steel, laminated wood and linoleum.

1926   F. Henri

42

BIOGRAPHIES AND CATALOGUE LIST

All works marked with an asterisk are illustrated in the catalogue

Joseph Albers (1888-1976)
Born in Bottrop in Germany, Albers first studied in Berlin 1913-15. He was a student and then a teacher at the Bauhaus, becoming influential with his designs for stained glass, typography and furniture, as well as painting and printing. After the Bauhaus closed in 1933, he settled in America and taught at the Black Mountain College in North Carolina and other institutions, where he continued to put into practice many of the Bauhaus ideas. Apart from his early work, he eschewed representation, making geometrical abstracts, which frequently consisted of a square painted with subtle tonal variations.

1 **Segments** 1934*
Woodcut, 23.2 x 28.2cm
Trustees of the British Museum
(Cambridge and Swansea only)

2 **"i"** 1934
Woodcut, 21.4 x 29.5cm
Trustees of the British Museum
(Liverpool and Kendal only)

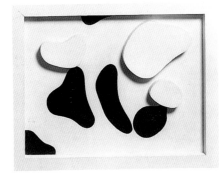

JEAN ARP **Constellation According to the Laws of Chance** c.1930, Tate Gallery, bequeathed by E C Gregory 1959 (cat. no. 3)

Jean (Hans) Arp (1886-1966)
Born in Strasbourg, Arp studied in Weimar and Paris. He was a co-founder of the Dada movement as well as being associated with Surrealism. He made abstract sculpture, collages and reliefs and published poems in German and French. From 1920 he lived mainly in Paris and in 1922 he married the artist Sophie Täuber, with whom he collaborated on experiments with cut paper compositions. He was a member of Abstraction-Création.

3 **Constellation According to the Laws of Chance** c.1930*
Painted wood relief, 54.9 x 69.8 x 3.8cm
Tate Gallery, bequeathed by E.C. Gregory 1959

Ella Bergmann-Michel (1896-1971)
Born in Paterborn in Germany, she studied in Weimar. In 1919 she married Robert Michel and moved with him to Vockenhausen. Her drawings reveal an interest in colour and forms and her abstract reliefs often incorporated unconventional materials such as silver paper and animal skins.

4 **Untitled** 1917*
Ink, wash and gold on paper, 71 x 50.4cm
Annely Juda Fine Art

5 **Untitled** c.1926
Ink and pencil on paper, 60 x 48.5cm
Annely Juda Fine Art

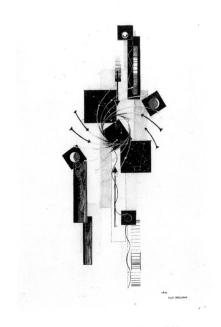

ELLA BERGMANN-MICHEL **Untitled** c.1926
Annely Juda Fine Art (cat. no. 5)

FLORENCE HENRI **Composition** 1926, University of East Anglia (cat. no. 13)

Charles Biederman (born 1906)
Born in Cleveland, Ohio of Czech parents. He studied in Chicago and moved to New York in 1934, where he began to make abstract paintings. In 1936 he visited Paris, where he saw Mondrian's work. When he was introduced to Constructivism by Pevsner, the organic shapes in his work gave way to geometrical ones. In his writings after the Second World War he argued that paintings should not contain any illusion of space, since a third dimension could be added in the form of a relief.

6 **Untitled 3** 1936*
Gouache on paper, 59 × 43cm
University of East Anglia

Sonia Delaunay-Terk (1885-1979)
Sonia Terk was born in the Ukraine and studied at Karlsruhe and Paris, where she later settled. After her marriage to Robert Delaunay in 1910, she collaborated with him on many projects, including the founding of Orphism, a more abstract, dynamic and colourful development of Cubism. Most of her works are brightly coloured abstracts and she later transferred some of the ideas of her paintings into designs for fabrics and clothes. She was a member of Abstraction-Création.

7 **Projet de Tissu** 1925*
Gouache on paper, 21 × 17.7cm
Annely Juda Fine Art

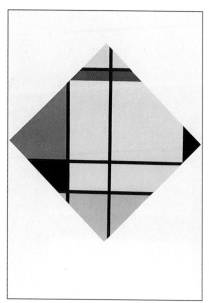

CÉSAR DOMELA **Lithographic Print** 1926/70
University of East Anglia (cat. no. 9)

8 **Untitled** 1925
Mixed media on paper, 47.5 × 27cm
Annely Juda Fine Art
(Swansea, Liverpool, Kendal only)

César Domela (born 1900)
Born in Amsterdam, Domela has spent most of his life in Paris. Self-taught, he began to make abstract work in 1923. He was active in the De Stijl movement in 1924-25, during which time he was influenced by Mondrian. He began to make reliefs while living in Berlin (1927-33). He was a member of Abstraction-Création and founded the magazine *Plastiques* with Arp and Täuber-Arp. He gradually incorporated more types of material into his reliefs and the delineations of form became increasingly more fluid.

9 **Lithographic Print** 1926/70*
Lithograph, 76.5 × 53cm
University of East Anglia

Naum Gabo (1890-1977)
The younger brother of the sculptor Antoine Pevsner, Gabo was born in Bryansk in Russia. He first studied medicine and civil engineering in Munich. On the outbreak of war in 1914, he moved to Norway where he made his first constructions in 1915, adopting the name Gabo to avoid confusion with his brother. He returned to Moscow in 1917, and in 1920 with Pevsner

NAUM GABO **Study for a Tower Fountain** 1924
Nina Williams (cat. no. 10)

published *The Realistic Manifesto* setting out his principles for a constructive
art. While living in Berlin from 1922 to 1932 he met the artists of the De Stijl
group and lectured at the Bauhaus. In 1926 Gabo and Pevsner designed the
set and costumes for Diaghilev's ballet *La Chatte*. Gabo joined Abstraction-
Création and also contributed to Cercle et Carré. In 1936 he moved to
Britain and edited *Circle* with Ben Nicholson and Leslie Martin. He spent
the war years in Cornwall and in 1946 emigrated to America, becoming a US
citizen in 1952. He was one of the first artists to experiment with kinetic
sculpture and employ transparent plastic in his work.

10   **Study for a Tower Fountain** 1924*
     Pencil on paper, 20.5 x 21cm
     Nina Williams

11   **Sketch for a Carving in Stone** 1930
     Crayon and gouache on paper, 27.3 x 33.7cm
     Nina Williams

12   **Construction in Space with Rose Marble Carving** 1966*
     Rose marble, mounted in perspex
     perspex frame 71 x 71 x 1cm; stone oval 45 x 33cm, variable depth
     Nina Williams

BARBARA HEPWORTH **Pierced Hemisphere** 1937, Wakefield Art Gallery (cat. no. 16)

Florence Henri (1895-1982)
Born in New York, Henri spent most of her life in France and was closely
associated with many of the major figures of European modernism. She
studied art and music in Paris, London, Rome and Munich. While in Paris she
studied with Léger. At the Bauhaus in 1928 she worked with Kandinsky, Klee
and Moholy-Nagy. After returning to Paris, she took up photography, taking
photographs of many of her artist friends.

13 **Composition** 1926*
Gouache on paper, 33.5 × 26.1cm
University of East Anglia

14 **Composition** 1927*
Ink and gouache on board, 55 × 45.8cm
University of East Anglia

Barbara Hepworth (1903-75)
Born in Wakefield, Hepworth studied at Leeds, before obtaining a scholarship
to the Royal College of Art. She learnt about marble carving while in Italy
with her first husband John Skeaping. On a visit to Paris with Ben Nicholson
(who became her second husband), she met Picasso and Mondrian. She
joined the Seven and Five Society in 1931 and Abstraction-Création and Unit
One in 1933. Her sculptures, although abstract, were often inspired by nature
and were mostly made by carving rather than modelling. She introduced into
Britain the use of the 'hole' in sculpture and, like Moore and Gabo, she used
stringing in some of her works. She moved to Cornwall with Nicholson at the
outbreak of the Second World War and remained there until her death.

15 **Conoid, Sphere and Hollow II** 1937*
Marble, 31.9 × 35.5 × 30.4cm
Government Art Collection

16 **Pierced Hemisphere** 1937*
Marble, 35 × 38 × 38cm
Wakefield Art Gallery

Auguste Herbin (1882-1960)
Born in Quiévy in France. Herbin studied at Lille and moved to Paris in 1903
where he spent some time working in isolation. After meeting Picasso and
Gris, he became influenced by Cubism and his paintings gradually became
more abstract. From 1926 onwards he was making completely abstract works.
He was a founder member of the group Abstraction-Création. His late works
consisted of compositions of geometrical shapes painted in pure unmodulated
colours.

17 **Abstract Composition** 1917
Gouache on paper, 50 × 32cm
University of East Anglia

IVAN KLIUN **Untitled** 1927-8
Annely Juda Fine Art (cat. no. 22)

Wassily Kandinsky (1866-1944)
Born in Moscow, where he studied law and political economy, before leaving to study painting in Munich in 1897. He wrote *On the Spiritual in Art* between 1910 and 1911 and started experimenting with abstraction. Although his earliest paintings were inspired by Russian folk art, he eliminated all representational forms from his later pictures, creating abstract compositions in pure colours, often on the analogy of musical compositions. He was instrumental in founding the *Blaue Reiter* group. Returning to Russia after the outbreak of the First World War, he became very active in artistic life and founded the INKhUK in 1920. He returned to Germany in 1921, joining the staff of the Bauhaus. After the Nazis came to power he settled in France and took French citizenship.

18 **Kleine Welten VI** 1922
Woodcut, 27.2 x 23.2cm
Trustees of the British Museum
(Liverpool and Kendal only)

19 **Kleine Welten XI** 1922*
Woodcut, 27.2 x 23.2cm
Trustees of the British Museum
(Cambridge and Swansea only)

Ivan Kliun (1873-1934)
Born in Kiev, where he began his artistic studies, Kliun later studied in Warsaw and Moscow. He began to make reliefs and sculptures in 1914 and subsequently contributed to important avant-garde exhibitions in Moscow, supporting Malevich's Suprematist ideas. In 1918 he participated in the design of decorations for the May Day celebrations. He taught at the Moscow State Free Art Studios and at the VKhUTEMAS and became a member of INKhUK.

20 **Untitled** 1920*
Watercolour on paper, 27 x 21cm
Annely Juda Fine Art

21 **Untitled** 1922*
Oil on carpet, 52.5 x 54cm
Annely Juda Fine Art

22 **Untitled** 1927-8*
Pencil on paper, 24.2 x 17cm
Annely Juda Fine Art

Gustav Klucis (1895-1938)
Born in Latvia, Klucis attended art school at Riga and St Petersburg, before joining the Ninth Latvian Infantry Regiment. Fighting for the Revolution, he travelled to Moscow where he sketched Lenin and participated in the design of decorations for the May Day celebrations of 1918. In the same year he entered the State Free Art Studios where he studied with Malevich. In 1920 he exhibited with Pevsner and Gabo. At this time he moved from making abstract paintings in a Suprematist style towards a greater interest in materials

and form. He turned these experiments to more utilitarian ends when he designed agitational stands and radio orators in 1922. From the mid-1920s he concentrated mainly on typography, photomontage and poster design. He was arrested and shot during the Stalinist purges.

23 **Colour Study** *c.*1920
Pencil, watercolour and ink on paper, 27 × 35cm
Annely Juda Fine Art

24 **Colour Study** *c.*1920
Pencil and watercolour on paper, 25 × 37.7cm
Annely Juda Fine Art

25 **Colour Study** *c.*1920
Ink and watercolour on paper, 26.7 × 20.9cm
Annely Juda Fine Art

26 **Architectural Study** *c.*1920-5*
Gouache, indian ink and pencil on paper, 39.5 × 24.8cm
Annely Juda Fine Art

Ivan Kudryashov (1896-1972)
Born in Moscow, he studied at the State Free Art Studios where he assimilated the principles of Suprematism from Malevich. In 1919 he moved to Orenburg where he was responsible for organising the local State Free Art Studios and where he produced and exhibited several designs for murals to embellish the town's theatre.

27 **Composition** 1921
Pencil on paper, 22 × 17.5cm
Annely Juda Fine Art

František Kupka (1871-1957)
Born in Opočno in eastern Bohemia, Kupka was apprenticed to a saddler before studying art at Jaromer, Prague and Vienna. He retained an interest in spiritualism and Theosophy throughout his life and, with Kandinsky, was one of the earliest artists to examine the spiritual symbolism of abstract colours and shapes. He also experimented with ways of suggesting movement through abstract forms, often in an analogy of music. He settled in Paris in 1896, where he worked as an illustrator as well as a painter. He later joined Abstraction-Création.

28 **Étude de Cercle** 1920
Gouache on card, 28 × 28cm
Adrian Heath

Bart van der Leck (1876-1958)
Born in Utrecht, van der Leck studied in Amsterdam. Although his early work was figurative, he began to paint abstract compositions and joined the De Stijl group after meeting Mondrian in 1916. His abstract works usually consist of geometrical shapes in red, yellow and blue on a white background. Whereas

GUSTAV KLUCIS **Architectural Study** *c.*1920-5
Annely Juda Fine Art (cat. no. 26)

Mondrian produced 'pure' abstract works, van der Leck's pictures frequently had an underlying figurative source. He also designed textiles, ceramics and interiors.

29 **Watercolour no. 390** c.1916-32*
Watercolour on paper, 34 x 27cm
University of East Anglia

El Lissitzky (1890-1941)

Born near Smolensk in Russia, El Lissitzky initially trained as an engineer. While teaching at the Vitebsk Art School in 1919 he came under the influence of Malevich and Suprematism. Subsequently he developed his concept of the PROUN (Affirmation of the New) as 'an interchange station between painting and architecture'; Proun was the title he gave all his abstract works. From 1922-5 he lived in Germany, Holland and Switzerland where he was an important promoter of International Constructivism. He continued to represent a significant means of communication between Russia and the West until the early 1930s. He worked extensively in book design, typography, exhibition layout (including the famous PROUN Room), photography and architecture.

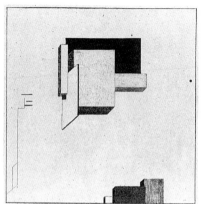

EL LISSITZKY **Proun 1C** 1919-21
Trustees of the British Museum (cat. no. 31)

30 **Proun IA** 1919-21*
Lithograph, 17 x 30cm
Trustees of the British Museum
(Cambridge and Swansea only)

31 **Proun IC** 1919-21*
Lithograph, 23.2 x 23.2cm
Trustees of the British Museum
(Cambridge and Swansea only)

32 **Proun, Unnumbered** 1919-21*
Lithograph, 30 x 23.8cm
Trustees of the British Museum
(Liverpool and Kendal only)

Kazimir Malevich (1878-1935)

Born in Kiev, Malevich studied in Moscow. Although his early paintings showed the influence of Cubism and Futurism, his own ideas soon became very influential and, with Mondrian he was the most important inaugurator of geometrical abstract painting. He was the founder of Suprematism, exhibiting his first Suprematist works in 1915 at the 0.10 exhibition in St Petersburg. These works contained abstract geometrical forms in pure colours against a white background often creating the impression of floating, falling and ascending. Apart from visits to Warsaw and Germany in 1927, he remained in Russia. His book, *The Non-Objective World*, was published by the Bauhaus in 1927 and brought his ideas to a wider audience.

33 **Suprematist Composition** c.1916*
Pencil on paper, 17 x 11.7cm
Annely Juda Fine Art

34 **Suprematist Composition** c.1916
Pencil on paper, 18.2 × 11cm
Annely Juda Fine Art

35 **Suprematist Composition** c.1920-2*
Oil on wooden panel, 61.8 × 29.7cm
Private Collection

Robert Michel (1897-1988)
Born in Vockenhausen, near Frankfurt in Germany. Michel's lifelong interest in
technical inventions is apparent in many of his works. Although his desire to
combine technology and art was very similar to the aims of the Bauhaus, he
was never a part of that school. He was in Berlin in 1922 for the First Russian
Exhibition and again in 1927. He travelled around Holland in 1927 with his
wife Ella Bergmann-Michel and Schwitters.

36 **Mécanique** 1924*
Mixed media on paper collaged on card, 38 × 48cm
Annely Juda Fine Art

37 **Ohne (variation 'Plein Pouvoir')** 1927-8
Mixed media and collage, 46.5 × 48.5cm
Annely Juda Fine Art

ROBERT MICHEL **Mécanique** 1924, Annely Juda Fine Art (cat. no. 36)

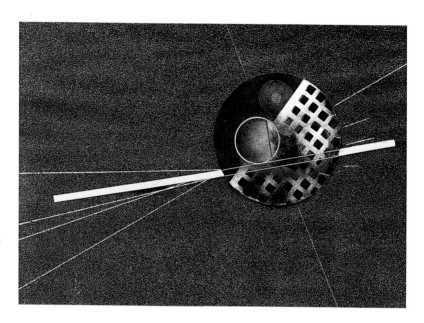

LÁSZLÓ MOHOLY-NAGY **Emery Paper Collage** 1930, Whitworth Art Gallery, University of Manchester (cat. no. 45)

László Moholy-Nagy (1895-1946)

After fighting in the First World War, Moholy-Nagy, a Hungarian law student, moved to Berlin to study art. He became acquainted with the work of Gabo, Malevich and El Lissitzky and in 1923 started teaching at the Bauhaus. He emigrated first to Amsterdam in 1934, then London in 1935. By 1937 he had moved to Chicago, where he founded a school called the 'New Bauhaus'. He worked extensively with new materials, including plexiglass and plastics, and he used semi-industrial techniques to produce his constructions. His abstract paintings from 1920 onwards show the influence of El Lissitzky and Malevich, with their squares and crossing diagonals. He also experimented with 'photograms' (painting with light), photography, stage design, documentary films and advertising designs.

38 **Composition** c.1921
Gouache and paper collage on paper, 49.5 x 35cm
University of East Anglia

39-44 **Konstruktionen** 1923
6 lithographs,
1: 59.7 x 43.8cm*
5: 59.9 x 43.7cm
6: 60.1 x 43.8cm
(Cambridge and Swansea only)
2: 60.1 x 43.8cm*
3: 60.1 x 43.7cm
4: 60.1 x 43.8cm*
Trustees of the British Museum
(Liverpool and Kendal only)

45 **Emery Paper Collage** 1930*
Collage with poster paint, 20.3 × 28.3cm
Whitworth Art Gallery, University of Manchester

46 **L + CH** 1936-9
Oil on canvas, 96.5 × 76.2cm
National Museum of Wales, Cardiff
(Cambridge and Swansea only)

Piet Mondrian (1872-1944)
Born at Amersfoort in the Netherlands, Mondrian studied in Amsterdam.
Early in his career he painted landscapes in the manner of The Hague School
and developed an interest in Theosophy, which was to affect his later
thinking. While living in Paris between 1911 and 1914 he became influenced
by Cubism. In 1917 he formed the De Stijl group with van der Leck and
van Doesburg and his work became increasingly abstract and rigorously geometrical, using only black, white, grey and primary colours. He lived in Paris
again from 1919 to 1938, before moving to London for two years. In 1940
he emigrated to America, where he exerted great influence on the New York
School.

47 **Composition with Red, Yellow and Blue** 1927*
Oil on canvas, 38 × 34.5cm
Private Collection

48 **Pier and Ocean (Study for the Pier at Scheveningen)** c.1914
Pencil on paper, 11.4 × 15.9cm
Annely Juda Fine Art
(Cambridge only)

Henry Moore (1898-1986)
Born in Yorkshire, Moore won a scholarship to the Royal College of Art.
During the 1930s he lived near Barbara Hepworth and Ben Nicholson in
Hampstead, but when his studio was bombed during the War, he moved
to Much Hadham in Hertfordshire. In 1930 he became a member of the
Seven and Five Society, and three years later he helped to form the avant-
garde group Unit One with Paul Nash. Although he experimented with semi-
geometrical abstraction in the 1930s, Moore's main concern was with the
human figure.

49 **Stringed Relief** 1937*
Bronze and string, length 47cm
The Henry Moore Foundation

50 **Head** 1937*
Green serpentine, height 33.5cm
The Henry Moore Foundation

Alastair Morton (1910-1963)
Born in Carlisle, Morton entered the family business of fabric production
and applied modern thinking to the design of textiles and interior design.

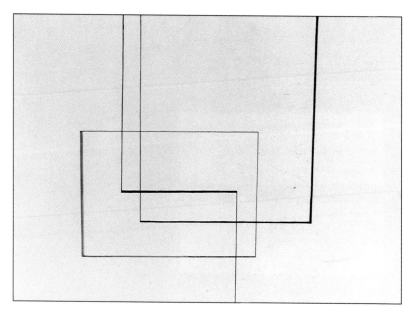

ALASTAIR MORTON **Drawing** 1940
University of East Anglia (cat. no. 51)

He founded the Edinburgh Weavers, becoming artistic director in the early 1930s. He used designs by Winifred Nicholson, Ben Nicholson and Barbara Hepworth, whom he had met at Brampton. He also painted and designed himself and was a supporter of contemporary art and architecture.

51 **Drawing** 1940*
Ink on paper, 25.4 x 35.5cm
University of East Anglia

Ben Nicholson (1894-1982)
Son of the painters William Nicholson and Mabel Pryde, Ben Nicholson was born in Denham. Apart from a brief period at the Slade School, he was self-taught. He visited Paris with his first wife, Winifred Nicholson in the early 1920s and later with his second wife, Barbara Hepworth in 1932, when he met Arp, Brancusi, Picasso, Miró and Calder. In 1933 he was introduced to Mondrian by Moholy-Nagy. His first abstract works were made in 1924. He exhibited regularly with the Seven and Five Society and joined Unit One and Abstraction-Création in 1933, the year in which he produced his first reliefs. In 1937 he edited *Circle* with J L Martin and Gabo. After the outbreak of the Second World War, he moved with Hepworth to Carbis Bay in Cornwall, where they were later joined by Gabo. He developed his own style of abstraction with subtle tones and lines, frequently based on still-lifes and landscapes.

52 **1935 (white relief)** *
Oil on carved board, 38 x 15.4cm
Private Collection

53 **1935 (painting)** *
Oil on canvas, 60 x 91cm
Private Collection

BEN NICHOLSON **1935 (painting)**, Private Collection (cat. no. 53)

Winifred Nicholson (1893-1981)
Born in Oxford, Winifred Roberts was the first wife of Ben Nicholson and
visited Paris with him in the early 1920s. In 1926 she began to exhibit regularly
in the Seven and Five exhibitions in London. She spent much time in Bankshead
in Cumbria, although she continued to travel extensively throughout her life.
In 1938 she persuaded Mondrian to leave war-torn Paris for London. She
painted abstract works only for a short period of time in the mid-1930s.

54 **Untitled** 1935-6*
Gouache on paper, 30.5 x 40.7cm
Raymond Danowski

Lyubov Popova (1889-1924)
Born near Moscow, Popova went to Paris to study in 1912, encountering works
by Cubist and Futurist artists. After returning to Russia she became an important
member of the Russian avant-garde, working in Tatlin's studio and contributing
to 0.10 and other important exhibitions. In 1916 she began to produce non-
objective works, which she described as 'Painterly Architectonics'. These works
were often characterised by dynamic circular forms with a subtle interplay of
colours. From 1922 she became increasingly involved with theatre and in 1924
she started making textile designs. She died prematurely of scarlet fever.

55 **Composition** 1917*
Oil on canvas, 84.5 x 66cm
Private Collection

56 **Composition** c.1920-1*
Gouache on card, 67.5 x 53.5cm
Annely Juda Fine Art

57 **Space-Force Construction** c.1920-1*
Oil on panel, 77.7 x 77.7cm
Private Collection

58 **Textile Design** 1924*
Pencil and coloured inks on paper, 23.4 x 19.1cm
Private Collection

Alexander Rodchenko (1891-1956)
Born in St Petersburg, Rodchenko was one of the pioneers of Constructivism.
In 1914 he moved to Moscow, where he became acquainted with the avant-
garde, including Malevich, Popova and Varvara Stepanova, whom he married.
In late 1915 he began to make experimental abstract works using a compass
and ruler and in 1918 made his first three-dimensional constructions. A founder
member of the First Working Group of Constructivists in 1921, during the
1920s he was also an important photographer and worked on stage and cos-
tume designs as well as typography for posters and films.

59 **Untitled** 1919*
Watercolour and oil on board, 49.5 x 35.5cm
Annely Juda Fine Art

LYUBOV POPOVA **Composition** c.1920-1, Annely Juda Fine Art (cat. no. 56)

KURT SCHWITTERS **Relief with Red Pyramid**
1923-5, Scottish National Gallery of Modern
Art (cat. no. 62)

Kurt Schwitters (1887-1948)
Born in Hanover, Schwitters studied at Dresden. In 1918 he created his own form of Dada called Merz, using rubbish materials such as bus tickets, broken wood etc in his collages and constructions. He published his poems and a magazine called *Merz*. The term Merz is meaningless and was invented by chance when fitting the letterhead of the Commerz und Privatsbank into a collage. He was friendly with Arp and van Doesburg and joined Abstraction-Création in 1932. He emigrated to Norway in 1937. After the German invasion of 1940, he fled to England, settling in Ambleside in the Lake District. He died in Kendal.

60 **Untitled** 1923
Lithograph, 56.6 x 44.5cm
Trustees of the British Museum
(Cambridge and Swansea only)

61 **Untitled** 1923
Lithograph, 55.8 x 44.4cm
Trustees of the British Museum
(Liverpool and Kendal only)

62 **Relief with Red Pyramid** 1923-5 *
Oil on wood relief, on plyboard, 60 x 50.2cm
Scottish National Gallery of Modern Art, Edinburgh
(Cambridge only)

63 **Collage** 1930 *
Paper collage, 17 x 13.2cm
Trustees of the British Museum
(Cambridge and Swansea only)

John Cecil Stephenson (1889-1965)
Born in Co. Durham, Stephenson studied at Leeds, the Royal College of Art and the Slade. He made his first abstracts in c.1932 and was producing uncompromisingly geometrical work by 1935. Mondrian, Nicholson, Hepworth and Moore were his neighbours in Hampstead and their presence no doubt helped formulate his own abstract work. Apart from art his other great interests were music and engineering.

64 **Untitled** c.1936/7 *
Gouache, ink and pencil on paper, 65.5 x 59.5cm
The Board of Trustees of the Victoria and Albert Museum

65 **Untitled** 1937 *
Gouache on paper, 13.4 x 11cm
University of East Anglia

66 **Drawing** 1939
Pencil, pen and gouache on paper, 43.4 x 26.5cm
University of East Anglia

Nikolai Suetin (1897-1954)

Born in the Kaluga district of Russia, Suetin served as a soldier at Vitebsk, where he later attended art school. It was there that he met Malevich, whom he later assisted with his Suprematist architectural constructions. From 1923 he worked at the State Porcelain Factory in St Petersburg where he decorated porcelain. In 1935 he painted Malevich's coffin with the 'Black Square'.

67 **Untitled** 1924-6*
    Watercolour on paper, 34 × 21cm
    Annely Juda Fine Art

Vladimir Tatlin (1885-1953)

Born in Moscow and raised in the Ukraine, Tatlin simultaneously embarked on two careers, both as an artist and a merchant sailor. In 1914 he visited Paris, where he met Picasso and saw his Cubist works. On his return to Russia he began to make entirely abstract three-dimensional reliefs. In 1915 he began to elaborate on the ideas of these first reliefs to create more dynamic constructions slung across corners, which he described as 'corner counter-reliefs'. He established the principle of Construction in these works which formed an essential basis for the development of Russian Constructivism. He was responsible for administering Lenin's Plan for Monumental Propaganda and in 1920 he built a tower of glass and wood called *Monument to the Third International*. He also produced designs for household items, clothes, the theatre and a flying machine.

Martyn Chalk's reconstructions of Tatlin's reliefs

Very few of Tatlin's reliefs have survived and most are known only from photographs. Tatlin used a variety of materials – tin, glass, wood etc with the aim of creating a three-dimensional relief rather than a pictorial space. The earlier reliefs stand out from a background while the 'corner counter-reliefs' of 1915-16 are fully three-dimensional. The following reconstructions are all by Martyn Chalk

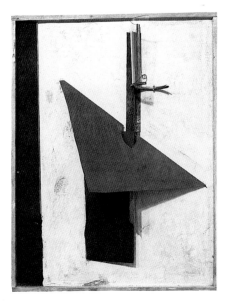

Reconstruction by Martyn Chalk 1981 of Tatlin's **Collection of Materials** 1914 Annely Juda Fine Art (cat. no. 70)

68 **Reconstruction of Tatlin's 'Painting Relief' 1913-4** 1982
    Wood, paper, pencil, gouache, wallpaper, etc., 60.5 × 29.2 × 6.6cm
    Annely Juda Fine Art

69 **Reconstruction of Tatlin's 'Painting Relief' 1913-4** 1982
    Wood, paper, gouache, oil paint, card, etc., 70 × 40 × 6cm
    Annely Juda Fine Art

70 **Reconstruction of Tatlin's 'Collection of Materials' 1914** 1981*
    Bitumen/sand mixture, iron, plaster, wood, glass, etc., 70 × 53.5 × 20cm
    Annely Juda Fine Art

71 **Reconstruction of Tatlin's 'Corner Counter-Relief' 1915** 1982
    Iron, wood, steel wire, cord, pulleys, etc., 225 × 232 × 82cm
    Annely Juda Fine Art

72 **Reconstruction of Tatlin's Counter-Relief *c.*1917** 1987*
    Wood, paint and steel treated with carbon and oil, etc., 73.5 × 40.5 × 16.5cm
    Annely Juda Fine Art

Sophie Täuber-Arp (1889-1943)
Born in Davos in Switzerland, Sophie Täuber trained as a dancer and textile
designer in Munich and was appointed professor of textile design at the
School of Applied Arts in Zürich in 1916 . She worked with a range of
materials on numerous projects, making abstract reliefs and paintings as well
as puppets and set designs. With van Doesburg and Arp, whom she married
in 1922, she created the decorations and design of Café de l'Aubette in
Strasbourg. She was a member of Abstraction-Création.

73 **Collage** c.1928*
Paper on card, 30.6 × 21.8cm
University of East Anglia

Paule Vézelay (1893-1984)
Born Marjorie Watson-Williams in Bristol, she adopted the name Paule
Vézelay after moving to Paris, where she lived from 1926 to 1939. She began
painting abstracts in about 1928, meeting Arp and Sophie Täuber-Arp
when she joined Abstraction-Création in 1934. She also made sculpture and
collages, designed fabrics and illustrated books.

74 **Grey Picture** 1935
Oil on canvas, 92 × 60cm
The artist's family

75 **Worlds in Space** 1935*
Oil on canvas, 81 × 100cm
The artist's family

Friedrich Vordemberge-Gildewart (1899-1962)
Born in Osnabrück in Germany, Vordemberge-Gildewart studied architecture
and sculpture in Hanover, where he met El Lissitzky. He also knew Arp,
Schwitters and van Doesburg and through the latter came into contact with
De Stijl. He was a member of Abstraction-Création. He left Nazi Germany in
1937 when non-representational art was proscribed. In 1938 he settled in
the Netherlands and became a Dutch citizen, although he later returned to
Germany. As well as painting, Vordemberge-Gildewart also made reliefs and
gave many of his works numbers instead of titles.

76 **Composition No. 60** 1931*
Oil on canvas, 25 × 40.5cm
Annely Juda Fine Art

*In the glossary and Russian biographies St Petersburg is used throughout although
the city was known 1914-1924 as Petrograd and 1924-1991 as Leningrad.*

SOPHIE TÄUBER-ARP **Collage** c.1928, University of East Anglia (cat. no. 73)

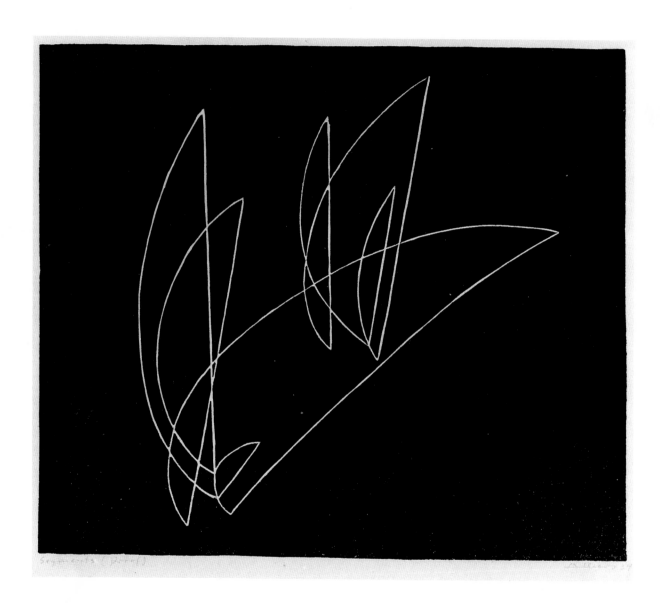

Segments (Proof)

GLOSSARY

Non-objective In English, this term has often been used to denote the complete absence of legible subject matter in a painting or sculpture, in preference to the more ambiguous 'abstraction', with its connotations of simplifying or in some other way transforming an observed or imagined image. It derives from the Russian 'Bespredmetnoe' as used by Malevich, and the German 'Gegenstandlöse'. Both more literally mean 'objectless' or 'without objects', implying the creation of a work of art from pure pictorial elements rather than from objects derived from the world of natural appearances. It is not associated with any particular group of artists or period in art.

Abstraction-Création *Abstraction-Création: – Art Non-Figuratif* was set up in Paris in 1931 to unite all practitioners of abstract art. It organised exhibitions and published an annual review, five issues of which appeared between 1932 and 1936. The cosmopolitan membership partly reflected the fact that by this time Paris had become an important centre of abstraction, with many foreign artists having taken refuge there. Although its composition changed, the group included Auguste Herbin (president), Georges Vantongerloo (vice-president), Jean Hélion (secretary) and Jean Arp (committee member), as well as César Domela, Sonia and Robert Delaunay, Naum Gabo, Barbara Hepworth, František Kupka, Piet Mondrian, Ben Nicholson, Antoine Pevsner, Kurt Schwitters, Paule Vézelay and Friedrich Vordemberge-Gildewart.

Bauhaus The Staatliches Bauhaus was set up in 1919 in Weimar by the architect Walter Gropius on the basis of fusing the existing School for Fine Art and the School for the Applied Arts. The initial Expressionist emphasis gave way after 1922 to an explicitly industrial approach to form and materials in tune with International Constructivism. The teaching staff included such figures as Klee, Kandinsky, Schlemmer and Moholy-Nagy. In 1926 the school moved to Dessau to purpose-built premises which served as a practical demonstration of Bauhaus principles. The school established firm links with mass production, but came under increasing pressure for its aesthetic and political radicalism particularly during the directorship of Hannes Meyer (1928-1930). It was subsequently moved to Berlin by Mies van der Rohe, its third and final director, and in 1933 was closed by the Nazis.

Circle *Circle: International Survey of Constructive Art*, edited by the painter Ben Nicholson, the sculptor Naum Gabo and the architect Leslie Martin, was published in 1937 by Faber and Faber, London. It was conceived as a periodical, but only one book-length issue appeared. It included articles by the editors, notable British avant-garde artists such as Barbara Hepworth and Henry Moore, as well as more international figures such as Piet Mondrian, Le Corbusier, Walter Gropius, László Moholy-Nagy and Lewis Mumford. Conceived partly to contest the influence of Surrealism, it promoted the 'constructive trend in current art, design and architecture'.

JOSEF ALBERS **Segments** 1934, Trustees of the British Museum (cat. no. 1)

Constructivism

Constructed sculpture, built up from separate elements of material rather than moulded or carved, was developed by Picasso and, in Russia, by Vladimir Tatlin around 1914. The term Constructivism was initially used in March 1921 by the First Working Group of Contructivists in Moscow, which included Alexander Rodchenko, Alexei Gan and Vavara Stepanova. Their aim was to participate in the construction of a post-revolutionary, socialist Russia, and they therefore rejected the autonomous art object in favour of adapting the elementary language of abstract art to designing everyday items for industrial production. In Western Europe, the International Faction of Constructivists set up in 1922 by Theo van Doesburg, Hans Richter and El Lissitzky disseminated a commitment to a clear and precise art that was collective rather than individualistic in its impulse. The international tendency of geometric abstract art, which has persisted ever since, is sometimes known as Constructivism.

Dada

Dada was essentially an international phenomenon that deliberately set out to shock the public, attacking aesthetic conventions and notions of good taste in all areas of the arts. It emerged between 1916 and 1917 in various centres: Zürich, Berlin, Cologne and New York and involved a wide range of artists and writers – the Germans: Hugo Ball, Hans Richter, Hannah Höch, Raoul Hausmann and Richard Huelsenbeck; the Rumanians: Tristan Tzara and Marcel and George Janco; the Frenchmen: Francis Picabia and Marcel Duchamp and the Alsatian: Jean Arp.

De Stijl

The De Stijl group was broadly committed to the aesthetic principles of Neo-plasticism and to the utopian aspiration of extending these principles into concrete material structures in the environment, with the aim of producing a more spiritual and harmonious society. It was a fluid grouping of artists, designers and architects, that included Theo van Doesburg, Piet Mondrian, Gerrit Rietveld, Vilmos Huszar, and Bart van der Leck, the architects J.J.P. Oud and Cornelius van Eesteren and the sculptor Georges Vantongerloo. The group was centred around the magazine *De Stijl* which was published in Holland 1917-1928 by van Doesburg.

INKhUK

The Institute of Artistic Culture was set up in Moscow in 1920, mainly by Kandinsky, who wrote its programme. Dedicated to investigating the language of art, the Institute rapidly moved away from the spiritual and psychological approach of its founder to a more materialistic ethos. In Spring 1921 the debate about the distinction between composition and construction let to the emergence of the First Working Group of Constructivists. From 1922 until its demise around 1924, the Institute was an important Constructivist think-tank.

Neo-plasticism

The term Neo-plasticism was coined by Piet Mondrian and the other Dutch artists of the De Stijl group to describe their art. A translation of the Dutch phrase 'de nieuwe beelding', it is nothing to do with plasticity in terms of tactile values in art, but rather with a new form of image making. This involved reducing the language of painting to the straight line, the right angle, the three primary colours (red, yellow and blue) and the three non-colours (black, white and grey).

Seven and Five Society This society was founded in 1920 on the principle, never actually followed, of exhibiting works by seven painters and five sculptors. By 1930, the dominant style was lyrical still-life and landscape painting. Following a ruling engineered by Ben Nicholson, the final exhibition of the society in October 1935 was the first in England to comprise only abstract work. It included Winifred Nicholson, Barbara Hepworth, Ivon Hitchens, Eric Holding, Arthur Johnson, Henry Moore, Roland Penrose, John Piper and Nicholson himself.

Suprematism Suprematism was developed by Kazimir Malevich in Russia during 1915 and launched in December that year when he exhibited 39 Suprematist paintings at the 0.10 (Zero-Ten) exhibition in St Petersburg. Suprematism, which he defined as 'the painting of pure form' and 'the supremacy of pure feeling', comprised dynamic configurations of geometric planes flatly painted against white grounds. Around 1918, Malevich painted his series of white on white paintings which create an even stronger sensation of immateriality and infinite space. In 1919 at Vitebsk he established a group called UNOVIS (Affirmation of the New in Art) which was dedicated to applying the principles of Suprematism to transform the environment.

Unit One *Unit One: The Modern Movement in English Architecture, Painting and Sculpture* was published in April 1934 in conjunction with an exhibition of the same name at the Mayor Gallery in London. The group were eclectic in approach, ranging from the poetic Surrealism of Paul Nash to the more abstract explorations of Ben Nicholson, Henry Moore, Barbara Hepworth and Eric Wadsworth.

VKhUTEMAS The State Free Art Studios were set up in Moscow in 1918 on the basis of the existing art schools. Tuition was free to all and students could choose their own teachers. Kandinsky, Malevich, Tatlin and Pevsner all taught at the Studios. In December 1920 the School was reorganised into the VKhUTEMAS, the Higher Artistic and Technical Workshops, which had a more disciplined and industrial orientation. Rodchenko, Popova, Stepanova, Klucis and later Tatlin and El Lissitzky were all involved in developing teaching programmes at the School in accordance with the tenets of Constructivism. The VKhUTEMAS was eventually closed in 1930.

L. Moholy-Nagy

FURTHER READING

General   A. H. Barr, *Cubism and Abstract Art*, New York, The Museum of Modern Art 1936, reprinted 1974

Harold Osborne, *Abstraction and Artifice in Twentieth Century Art*, Oxford, Clarendon Press 1979

Towards a New Art: Essays on the Background to Abstract Art 1910-20, London, Tate Gallery 1980

Magdalena Dabrowski, *Contrasts of Form: Geometric Abstract Art 1910-1980*, New York, Museum of Modern Art 1985

Anna Moszynska, *Abstract Art*, London, Thames and Hudson 1990

Mark A. Cheetham, *The Rhetoric of Purity: Essentialist Theory and the Advent of Abstract Painting*, Cambridge University Press 1991

Suprematism   L. Zhadova, *Kazimir Malevich: Suprematism and Revolution in Russian Art 1910-1930*, London, Thames and Hudson 1982

De Stijl   Hans L. Jaffé, *De Stijl*, London, Thames and Hudson 1970. (A useful introduction and selection of translated texts).

Mildred Friedman (ed.), *De Stijl 1917-1931: Visions of Utopia*, Oxford, Phaidon 1982

Paul Overy, *De Stijl*, London, Thames and Hudson 1991

Constructivism   Stephen Bann, (ed.), *The Tradition of Constructivism*, London, Thames and Hudson 1974

Christina Lodder, *Russian Constructivism*, London and Newhaven, Yale University Press 1983

Art into Life, Russian Constructivism 1914-1932, Seattle, Henry Art Gallery and New York, Rizzoli 1990

Bauhaus   Hans M. Wingler, *The Bauhaus: Weimar, Dessau, Berlin, Chicago*, Cambridge Massachusetts, MIT 1969

Frank Whitford, *Bauhaus*, London, Thames and Hudson 1984

France   *Abstraction-Création*, Paris, Musée d'Art Moderne de la Ville de Paris 1978

Britain   Naum Gabo, Leslie Martin, Ben Nicholson, *Circle*, London, Faber and Faber 1937, reprinted 1971

Charles Harrison, *English Art and Modernism 1900-1939*, London, Allen Lane 1981

Circle, Cambridge, Kettle's Yard 1982

LÁSZLÓ MOHOLY-NAGY **Konstruktionen** 1923, Trustees of the British Museum (cat. no. 42)

COPYRIGHT

Inside back cover BEN NICHOLSON AND BARBARA HEPWORTH
Courtesy Tate Gallery Archives